# Learning to Sleep in the Middle of the Bed

*poems by*

# Alexis Cameron Stark

*Finishing Line Press*
Georgetown, Kentucky

# Learning to Sleep in the Middle of the Bed

Copyright © 2021 by Alexis Cameron Stark
ISBN 978-1-64662-506-2 First Edition
All rights reserved under International and Pan-American Copyright Conventions. No part of this book may be reproduced in any manner whatsoever without written permission from the publisher, except in the case of brief quotations embodied in critical articles and reviews.

## ACKNOWLEDGMENTS

"My Umbrella is An Introvert." *East Lansing Art Festival Poetry Press*, 4th edition, 2019.

Publisher: Leah Huete de Maines
Editor: Christen Kincaid
Cover Art: SeeJaneRun, LLC
Author Photo: Erin Albanese
Cover Design: Elizabeth Maines McCleavy

Printed in the USA on acid-free paper.
Order online: www.finishinglinepress.com
also available on amazon.com

Author inquiries and mail orders:
Finishing Line Press
P. O. Box 1626
Georgetown, Kentucky 40324
U. S. A.

# Table of Contents

Honesty Poem ............................................................................ 1

My Umbrella Is an Introvert .................................................... 3

My Mom's 90's Sweater ............................................................ 5

Super-patriarchal-color-me-heteronorma-docious .............. 7

Fireflies ....................................................................................... 9

Freedom ................................................................................... 10

Intuition ................................................................................... 11

Mantra for Recovery .............................................................. 12

Red Light, Green Light .......................................................... 14

Title, Undecided ...................................................................... 15

My Poor Therapist .................................................................. 17

Your First, My Middle ............................................................ 18

Meditations on Grief: In Two Parts ...................................... 19

Trust Issues ............................................................................. 22

Hurricane ................................................................................. 23

Learning to Sleep in the Middle of the Bed ........................ 24

Jostled ...................................................................................... 25

Serenity Prayer ....................................................................... 26

Church in the Wild ................................................................. 28

Sunsets are an Act of Self-care ............................................. 29

Writer's Cramp ....................................................................... 30

*This book was made from love and hate. Trust and doubt.
It exists thanks to those who love her and
her own bravery to keep climbing mountains.
Let these stories serve as someone else's survival guide.*

**Honesty Poem**

Sometimes,
I need to use nose spray
to fall asleep at night.
Sleep also requires an oscillating fan
blowing cold air and at least
four fuzzy blankets.

Sometimes, all the time,
I write on sticky notes reminding me
to do laundry, send that email,
shower, eat dinner, love yourself
as much as you love your mom.
To look up inspirational
videos or songs that
won't make you feel sad or
words from God telling you
to have faith, let go, and
watch your enemies
fall behind you.

If we're being honest,
I kill cacti.
I can't keep plants alive
no matter how pretty they are,
because it's hard to provide water
and sunshine when you're still
trying to find them for yourself.

At work, I wear glasses
in front of screens to protect
my eyes from burning blue light.
Sometimes, I keep them on long after
the laptop is shut to protect
my soul from being seen and
getting burned beyond repair.

When I'm honest, I'll tell you
I have a nervous bladder in bathroom stalls.
I eat sprinkles out of the jar.
I don't always stop at stop signs.
I can't keep both eyes fully open in pictures.
I love driving with the windows down,
but I hate the sound of the wind when it whips.

Sometimes I forget to pee.
I forget to eat too.
I've trained my mind to tune out signals
from my body, renamed calls for help
as progress and success.

## My Umbrella is an Introvert

People don't deserve umbrellas.

Household objects,
destined to serve humans.
None are like the umbrella.

Rain jackets are extroverts.
Wearing their hearts on their sleeves,
their bright, flashy colors protect their humans
from the elements, wanting to be worn even
when it's not raining.
Sometimes spread too thin,
they allow rain to seep down thighs,
into soggy sneakers.

Ponchos have personal space issues.
Their extensive yardage of plastic
envelops the entire human. A simple hug
seems calming and dry until
you're suffocating.

Umbrellas are soldiers.
When rain clouds and thunderstorms
crawl into town, the umbrella is the
first to bear arms.

Nobody ever asks the umbrella,
"Do you feel like opening up today?"
"Do you want to go outside?"
It's assumed the umbrella will be ready
and willing to keep the rain from
chilling scalps and shirts from
clinging to chests.

Umbrellas are fragile.
Sure, they'll listen to your troubles
and groans while trudging through
puddles on the way to class,
late for the second time this week.

Introverts are good for that.
They keep the rain off others
don't focus on their own
clothes getting soaked.

Easier to let tears run down
nylon, spindly wires,
the outside of the umbrella,
than to cry on the inside.

In closets, under passenger's seats
umbrellas thrive. Away from people
and the gregarious outside world.
But when duty calls,
Umbrellas are there.

Umbrellas are always there.

## My Mom's 90's Sweater

Cleaning out the old and dusty
80's polyester explosion
from her closet,
my mom tossed aside a black
and white
and beige
knit sweater.
It is rare I find beauty
in my mom's clothing,
items usually older than me
and worn well over 30 years
in one tall glass building off I-75.

Not soft,
not pretty,
but it held a piece of her,
like a secret
in the yarn,
wound together as tight as I am.
Refusing to unravel.

I am wound the way
I watched my mother wind,
knit one, pearl two,
knit three, pearl four, five,
20 years.

My birth stone is a pearl.

Her sweater scratches
the back of my neck,
keeping my chin up,
like my mother and
her mother and
her mother before her
says when I'm down.

I took the sweater.
She was just going to throw it away.
She wasn't attached to it.

Now I am attached
to my 90s sweater,
the decade I was born and made
my mother a mom.

## Super-patriarchal-color-me-heteronorma-docious

We judge sunsets by the
magentas and oranges splashed
across the horizon. How long they can
hold their breath before giving into
the navy and periwinkle night.

We judge apples by the
color of their skin.
Red Delicious, superior to
sour, crotchety Granny Smith.
Yellow ones are antisocial.
No one really talks about them.

From the moment humans are born,
we judge them by anatomy and
define them by pink and blue.

What a way to determine a color.
During that final push,
red stained, white scrubs
deciding the fate of a human.

A fate involving walking into Babies R Us,
your tiny hands pulled
one way or the other.
Towards khakis and jean overalls
or sparkly, flowery jumpers,
all based on the color you were
assigned at birth.

Hot Wheels flames painted
red and black, too dark and dangerous
for Barbie or Cinderella.
Barbie, in her pink mini skirt, forced to ride
in Ken's blue sports car, when she really
wants to kick it with Wonder Woman
for date night at the dream house.

Dependency on social norms,
built tall and strong like the
fashionista shopping mall your daughter
will build out of pink and purple
Lego Friends sets.
Costs just a few cents more for a mom,
who makes a few cents less.

**Fireflies**

Written in a quiet room,
from a noisy, cluttered mind.
Bound for books or maybe
just bound to never leave
that room or catch themselves
on the doorway.
They tangle around my knuckles
gasping for air, scampering
up my hands and wrists,
down my shoulders
like fireflies.
From the tip of the pen
onto the page,
like lightning.

**Freedom**

Roger was mine.
I spent hours cleaning
and fixing
and planning
and dreaming
of being reckless
because I had a truck
and an FM radio.

**Intuition**

I dreamt the RV was on fire.

The windows cracked,
smoke spilling out.
The leather-covered seats
split and cracked around the
curve of the steering wheel.

No one was inside.
No one around
to watch it burn.

Except me.
I saw it all.
I watched the metal melt,
the vehicle slowly become
unrecognizable.
A warped tin can that
used to be someone's home.

Like something melting without your consent.

Waking up in cliché cold sweats,
I questioned my dream.
No one hurt.
Nothing destroyed.
Yet I was still sweating.

I questioned
why I worried.
Why I didn't drop everything,
run for water,
to put out the fire.

Intuition told me
I needed to learn
to watch things burn.

**Mantra for Recovery**

Intrusive thoughts
run on treadmills
refusing to slow.

It gets better.

Bottled up,
like the prescription
you don't want to take.

One hour,
an eternity.
You learn to
celebrate the
little victories.

Surrendering to recovery,
rough like sandpaper,
sanding away layer by layer.
Bone deep

like nails in palms
on a cross,
where your savior
made His sacrifice.

A Rubik's cube
stacked tight.
You try to
solve the puzzle faster,
only feeling more confused.

Moving fast, nothing changing.

The gold chain tightens
around your neck.
His reigns pulling you back.

Ease up, let go,
unclench fists,
raise hands upward.
Falling on your knees,
asking for help,
a sign of strength.

Scratching, screaming, solving.
Falling, praying, believing
it does get better.

## Red Light, Green Light

Today,
I am afraid my
office chair is counting
the ways it could break down
and dump me on the floor.
Like it just didn't feel like
holding me up anymore.

I guess the fall
wouldn't be too bad.
Unless the floor
gives up too.

I place the faith of God
into anything remotely sturdy.
Not just in
chairs and floors
but in love and
microwaves,
sandwiches,
and traffic lights.

Traffic lights should hang
over every choice I make.
The light could turn red when
the floor is about to cave in
and I would know it is time
to stop.

**Title, Undecided**
    *"You ever decide, by not deciding?"* —Neil Hilborn

You sat with me,
on the stained college carpet stairs
and waited.
Watched me unravel
the freshly wound hiking boot laces,
scheming to trip me
and watch me fall.

*Just pick one.*

In the moment it felt practical
to be caught between
color and cost and comfort.

You sat down next to me and
I wondered if the ground in Alaska
would be as forgiving as you.

More supportive than my ankle,
which I was certain would give out
while hiking up mountains so
I should choose the one with
the most arch support even
though they're more money.

I thought the cheaper ones were
"good enough" and it's no surprise
I almost picked them because
I don't think I deserve better than
"good enough."

So, I spent more time sitting,
on the stairs with deadlocked pros and cons.

I was scared of choosing the wrong boots.
I was scared of climbing mountains in the wrong boots.
I was scared of climbing mountains.

When my heavy head finally
sank between my knees,
you untied both boots.
Removed the weight from my feet.

You moved mountains for me.
I made more,
deciding not to decide.

## My Poor Therapist

For breakfast I had cereal with
Milk spilled out of all corners of my bed
Waking up dehydrated after dreaming about
Murders and math problems for a
Test of endurance as I put on my scarf to go
Outside my comfort zone for choosing not to text
Goodnight is closure to my day and when
It doesn't happen, I brush my teeth after getting out of
The bed feels itchy, so I take off my scarf when I get
Inside of my own head during class, in the car
On the way to therapy and when I
Get to class I have 12 tabs open to
Keep me focused on driving and thinking
About what that one author meant when
They said they loved me but didn't text
Goodnight only comes after the work is
All done. By the time I pull in the parking lot
I have a list of what I'm going to say and
Do all day so when I come to you it's all
Figured out and I can say I'm just
Finally, able to sit down for 5 minutes to
Breathe and let the milk
Spill out.

**Your First, My Middle**

Wandering
though Meijer,
I pick up a bag of coffee.

The name,
your first, my middle,
brought back all the
hard-to-swallow beans
I thought I'd managed
to grind into coffee
and finish the cup of
lingering bitterness,
before anyone could notice
you burned my tongue.

## Meditations on Grief: In Two Parts

I

Grief is not a flat surface; it's broken.
No matter how many times
you try to fit the old pieces
back together. No matter
how many times you try
to paint over it, give it a fresh
new coat, glossy finish,
good as new. It will never be.

Grief makes dry ground crack,
like the sound of blown out car speakers.

Abrupt
like slipping on the slick shower floor,
slamming your forehead into
the side of the sink.
Your senses can't distinguish
bleeding from crying.
Both come so easily,
quietly.

Waves don't always come wailing,
rushing with storm warnings.
They come in fine lines between
feeling better and
getting unfriended on Facebook.

Flat is failure.
Grief is mountains.

You kill yourself climbing,
sweating,
staying hydrated,
well rested, fed, dressed, healthy,
clean face, dry mascara.
Throwing black-brown stained, soggy pieces
of paper towel in the trash,
check the mirror before unlocking the door.
Because you can't let them know
you're climbing mountains.
Because when they look at you,
they only see the
flat ground you're walking on,
putting your best foot forward,
one in front of the other.

Moving forward
doesn't mean
you've moved on.


II

I am waiting
for paint to dry.
For the power to come back on.
Electrical wires down, but in a few hours
the lights will turn back on.

You know they will.

In the meantime,
you're left in silence, darkness,
absence of light and sound with that thing
you're missing. That thing

that keeps you driving on endless
stretches of road at night.
Pressing the gas to the floor,
knowing you're almost there but
you're anxious. You don't know
how much longer you can stay awake.

Grief isn't linear or lazy.
It's learning to love yourself
despite the lingering longing you feel.
The constant patching up of those
parts of you that feel like
they're missing.

Feeling air slowly escaping
from your back-bike tire when
you're just trying to get somewhere,
away from where you've been.

**Trust Issues**

At night
I dream about
running through
dark spaces,
hallways with doors.

*Keep the faith.*
I run into walls.
*Trust the process.*
Doors slam.

Falling down
isn't safe when
you can't see
the ledge to
pull yourself
back up.

I wake up and
my hand goes
to grip my
collarbone,
to make sure
my tattoo
is still there.

To make sure
it didn't fall off
and get lost
in the dark.

I wake up and
question permanent ink.

And you wonder
why I have
trust issues.

## Hurricane

I asked God to help me grow
in my ability to be alone.
I expected him to mail me
a packet of seeds with
instructions on how to plant
and water and wait for growth.

Instead he sent a storm.

The swollen raindrops stung
pelting on my skin,
like dropping coins on toes.

The roar of thunder, louder
than my yelps and
"welp, this isn't what I wanted."

The rain carried away
all the weeds around me,
leaving my roots strong
and lonely.

Rainbows come after rain,
hanging over your head
even when you don't notice.

Light shines through
when you realize God's plan
was to make you clean
and let you learn
how to grow strong
and tall,
alone.

## Learning to Sleep in the Middle of the Bed

My therapist uses a whiteboard
to draw me a river,
show me where I should be floating
between the banks of rigidity and chaos.

It's uncomfortable.
Moving towards a happy medium
feels extreme.

I sleep on the right side of the bed,
on the edge, leaving
over half of the bed untouched.
At some point, I unconsciously
decided I don't deserve
the whole bed all to myself.

Now the bed is mine, no one else's.

I'm slowly learning
to take up space.
Uncross my legs on buses and
church pews and couches.
Be present in a room,
an undeniable force
instead of an inconvenience
taking up space.

Generously applying lotion
to my entire body because
the whole bottle is mine.
Speaking up, claiming
the last piece of pizza or cookie,
instead of floating to the back
waiting for someone braver,
bolder, to make the first move.

Asking for what I need
even when I'm sleeping on the edge,
thinking I am not deserving of excess
in a world harboring deficit.

**Jostled**

The dog
scampered
around the corner,
bumping into the
table with the fishbowl.

The goldfish
sloshed around
in the water,
but the bowl
did not fall.

The bowl
was not broken.
All the pebbles and
plants and the
Goldfish remained
un-spilled.

She was just
jostled.

## Serenity Prayer

> *"God, grant me the serenity*
> *to accept the things I cannot change,*
> *the courage to change the things I can,*
> *and the wisdom to know the difference."*

Lord,
grant me the strength
to let the ruin
end here.

Courage,
to know the difference
between bravery and
self-destruction.

Wisdom,
to accept
I am blind
to all things beyond
the reach of my arms
and the length
of my stride.

Life,
because I know
I am not as broken
as the one
who broke me.

Acceptance,
of the tangible,
casting aside
figments of my
expectations.

Sin,
to steer my ship
straight,
out of the storm
instead of resisting
surrender.

Peace,
in saying Amen
and knowing
thy will be done.

## Church in the Wild

On the
first day
there
was light,
followed
by earth
and rivers,
day and
night, and
it was good. Because He said it was. On the seventh day,
He rested; on the eighth, He went to the gym. He made bibles
and barbells, found sanctuary in sit-ups and squats. Lifting
strengthened His shoulders to carry the new world.
He broke
down to
be rebuilt;
let it hurt,
then let it go.
Tied his
shoes, fixed
his ponytail,
so His crown
wouldn't slip.
Breathed in.
Breathed out.
And it was good.

**Sunsets are an Act of Self-care**

The Sun runs away to the
sands of Lake Michigan,
like she knows to come out west
because she needs wide open spaces
to explode, like pinecones scream
when they catch fire.

In the morning
she rises again
with a grateful heart,
shining light in the places
that have gone dark.

She's not afraid of
getting lost in the dark,
only of losing herself.

The Sun doesn't hide
out of fear, she's just resting,
preparing to rise the next day
with grace.

## Writer's Cramp

If my pen could write my essay for me,
maybe my clothes would make it into
my closet instead of decorating my floor.
Maybe my dishes would finally make it
from the counter to the sink.

If my essay was written for me
then where would my words go?

Trapped alone in my own head
all twisted, dark, dressed up, nowhere to go.

Getting the pen in my hand is easy.
Forcing the pen to explain
how and why and
when I decided creating art was
more important than money,
is the challenge.

My letters learned to run
together, tripping over the
perilous practice of cursive
I learned when I was six but
never saw the importance
in committing to memory.

If only a plastic stick and metal tip
could move as fast as the storylines
racing through your head.

As a writer, I'm expected
to be the storyteller for those
too busy to take notes and
a voice for those too
oppressed to make waves.

To live in constant fear that
one day the pen in my hand
will turn on me and
gouge my eyes out.

The future rests in hands
mutilated by paper cuts and
crumpled up ideas of how to
change the world and leave my
name written somewhere
in permanent marker
instead of pencil.

Between the lines of her professional writing, Alexis finds the words to share her own stories through poetry. From her green years of scribbling streams of childhood consciousness in notebooks, to her green and white years of interning with the Center for Poetry at Michigan State University, Alexis used words to navigate her journeys. During her college years, she created and facilitated arts and poetry workshops for incarcerated men at prisons in Michigan, exploring the potential of arts to create positive social change and promote individuality within the prison system. Today, she tells stories about people to bring joy in the darkness and truth amid injustice through her career as a journalist.

A metro Detroit native, she traveled progressively west across Michigan, following route I-96, from MSU to Grand Rapids. There she found work, friendships, a few good beers, and a nest just a short drive from Lake Michigan. Writing continues to be her safe haven, alongside her family, Disney movies, and her very comfortable bed.

www.ingramcontent.com/pod-product-compliance
Lightning Source LLC
LaVergne TN
LVHW041602070426
835507LV00011B/1251

*9781646625062*